© 1990 Franklin Watts

Franklin Watts Inc
387 Park Avenue South
New York, NY 10016

Printed in Belgium

Designed by
K and Co

Photographs by
NASA
TASS
British Aerospace
Aerospatiale

Technical Consultants
L.J. Carter
S. Young

Library of Congress Cataloging-in-Publication Data

Barrett, Norman S.
     The picture world of space shuttles / Norman Barrett.
          p.   cm. — (Picture World)
     Summary: Describes how space shuttles work and looks at various missions.
     ISBN 0-531-14056-3
     1. Space shuttles—Juvenile literature. [1. Space shuttles.]
I. Title. II. Series.
TL795.5.S733 1990
629.44'1—dc20   89-21540
                                                           CIP AC

The Picture World of

Space Shuttles

N. S. Barrett

CONTENTS

Franklin Watts

New York • London • Sydney • Toronto

Introduction

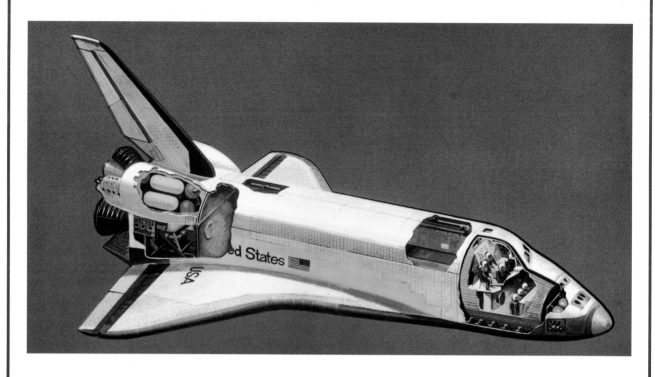

Space shuttles are spacecraft that can be reused. They take off like a rocket, orbit the Earth like a spacecraft and land like a plane.

The United States has been operating space shuttles since 1981. Their uses include launching satellites and carrying out experiments in space.

The first Soviet shuttle was launched in 1988. Other shuttles are being planned by the European Space Agency and by Japan.

△ A cutaway picture of the U.S. space shuttle showing its rocket engines at the back and the flight deck and working quarters at the front. The middle section is the cargo bay. American space shuttles usually carry five to seven astronauts.

▷ The proposed European space shuttle, *Hermes*, scheduled for operation in the late 1990s.

◁ The Soviet space shuttle *Buran* on the launch pad. Its first flight, in November 1988, was unmanned.

Enterprise

The decision to build a space shuttle was made in the 1970s. The National Aeronautics and Space Administration (NASA) chose the final design from several ideas. It involved a large fuel tank and rockets that could be separated when used up.

A special orbiter, the part that would orbit the Earth and return, was built for tests. It was called *Enterprise*, after the spaceship in the television series *Star Trek*.

▽ The public gets a first glimpse of the orbiter *Enterprise*, in 1976. *Enterprise* did not have working engines, so it never went into space.

△ *Enterprise* is rolled out fixed on top of a specially adapted Boeing 747 airliner for gliding and landing trials.

▷ After riding "piggyback" on the jumbo jet, *Enterprise* was released at a height of 7 km (4.3 miles). Two astronauts piloted it safely down and made a successful landing.

First flights

The first true space shuttle was *Columbia*, which made its first flight in 1981. The first four *Columbia* flights, all piloted by a crew of two, were trials. Various systems and maneuvers were tested.

During the 1980s, three more orbiters were built, *Challenger*, *Discovery* and *Atlantis*. In 1986, on the 25th shuttle launch, *Challenger* tragically blew up soon after take-off on its own tenth flight.

△ The first shuttle launch. *Columbia* takes off from the launch pad at Kennedy Space Center with its massive external fuel tank and rocket boosters attached.

▷ The two solid rocket boosters are cast off after about two minutes, when their fuel is used up. The empty fuel tank is also jettisoned, when the shuttle reaches the edge of space.

◁ The empty rocket boosters are recovered at sea after parachuting down from about 45 km (28 miles). The used fuel tank will have broken up in the atmosphere.

▷ *Columbia* completes a successful first trip as it touches down at Edwards Air Force Base, California, one of the three landing sites for shuttles in addition to Kennedy Space Center.

Up in space

Most shuttle missions have a crew of five to seven — a commander, pilot, mission specialists and sometimes payload specialists.

The commander and pilot control the orbiter from the flight deck, where there are also controls and displays for special missions. The mid-deck area includes the galley and food storage and the sleeping stations. The lower deck contains the equipment for cleaning and controlling the air supply.

△ Commander Vance Brand (right) and pilot Robert Overmyer on the flight deck of *Columbia* during the fifth shuttle flight.

▷ The payload bay doors remain open while the shuttle is in orbit. The manipulator arm can be seen to the left, while sunshields cover the empty satellite cradles.

▽ An astronaut, attached to the manipulator arm, has just released a satellite into orbit.

NASA shuttle flights average six to eight days. During this time the orbiter makes about 90 to 125 orbits of Earth.

Spacesuits are not normally needed in the working and living quarters. Conditions are made as comfortable as possible for the astronauts. Food is served on trays like those used on airliners. The crew usually sleeps at the same time, in sleeping bags.

▽ Astronauts at work inside the orbiter. Pilot "Rick" Hauck is at the flight controls (left). Sally Ride, the first American woman in space, and Norman Thagard were mission specialists on *Challenger* during this seventh shuttle flight. Seats are not needed because in space astronauts are weightless.

Mission control

Each shuttle flight is planned years ahead. The astronauts train for months for their particular jobs and missions. During the flight they are in constant radio contact with mission control on the ground.

Mission control has specialists to monitor all the shuttle's systems and the astronauts themselves. There are even doctors who conduct medical interviews with each astronaut.

△ Mission control, surprisingly, is not based at the Kennedy Space Center, where the launch takes place, but in Houston, Texas. About seven seconds after take off, Houston takes over from ground control at Cape Canaveral.

Shuttle highlights

NASA conducted 24 successful shuttle flights between April 1981 and January 1986 before *Challenger* blew up. This tragedy halted the shuttle program for over 2¹/₂years.

Flights resumed in September 1988. They have been planned for several years ahead, with up to 14 a year. A new orbiter to replace *Challenger* is scheduled for 1992, called *Endeavor*.

△ The first shuttle roll-out. *Columbia* moves slowly to the launch pad for its first flight in 1981. The shuttle is prepared for launch in the vehicle assembly building and carried from there by a crawler-transporter running on special gravel tracks.

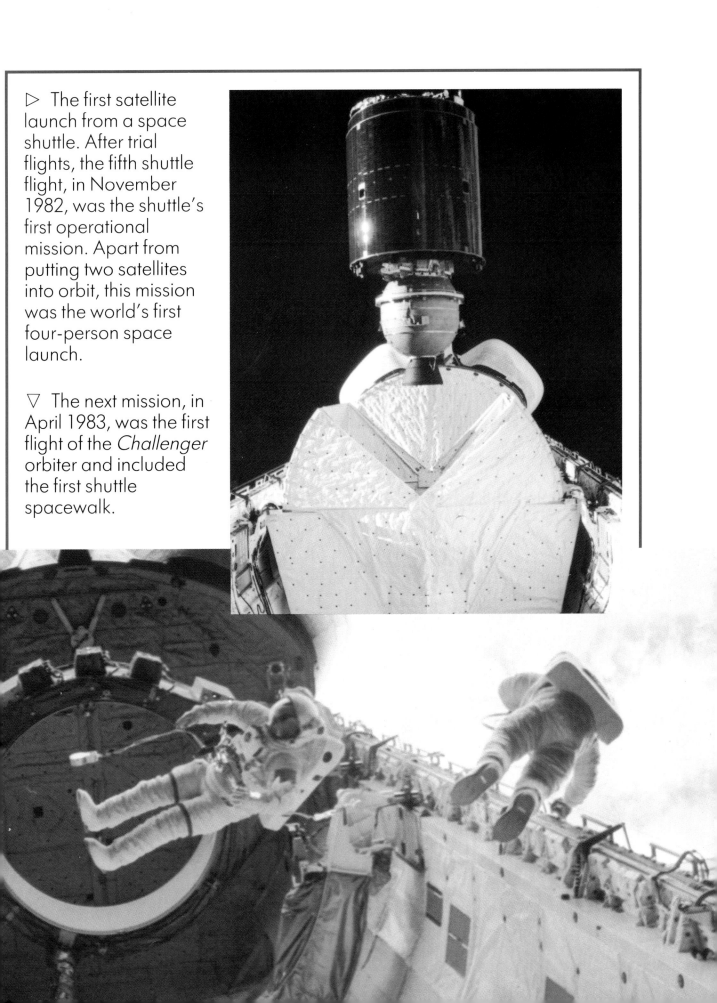

▷ The first satellite launch from a space shuttle. After trial flights, the fifth shuttle flight, in November 1982, was the shuttle's first operational mission. Apart from putting two satellites into orbit, this mission was the world's first four-person space launch.

▽ The next mission, in April 1983, was the first flight of the *Challenger* orbiter and included the first shuttle spacewalk.

Some shuttle flights are reserved mainly for carrying a scientific laboratory called *Spacelab*. This is a project developed for NASA by the European Space Agency (ESA).

Spacelab is a set of modules 2.7 m (8.9 ft) long which fit into the cargo bay and are connected to the shuttle airlock by a tunnel. Scientists, or payload specialists, work in *Spacelab* conducting zero-gravity and other experiments.

▷ The first launch of the orbiter *Discovery*, in August 1984. This was the 12th shuttle flight.

▽ Scientist-astronauts working in *Spacelab* on its first flight on the *Columbia* shuttle in November 1983. *Challenger* took up Spacelab three times in 1985. Further flights are planned for the 1990s.

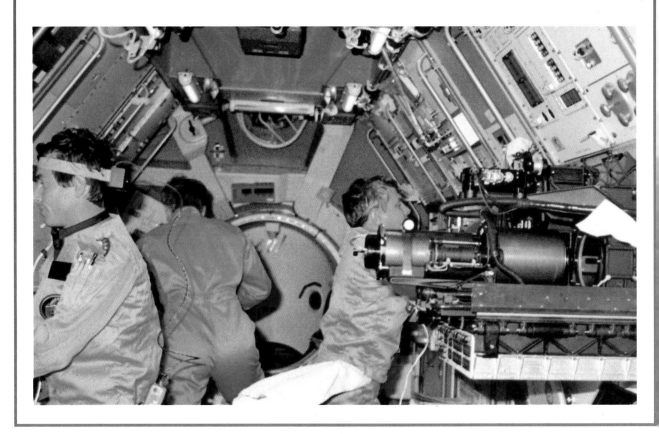

◁ Astronauts working on a satellite in the *Challenger* cargo bay, in April 1984. This was the first repair of a satellite in orbit.

▷ The first launch of *Atlantis*, the fourth shuttle, in 1985.

▽ An astronaut retrieves one of the two satellites rescued by *Discovery* in November 1984. The satellites, whose engines had failed to work, were returned to Earth in the shuttle.

Other shuttles

The Soviet Union's first space shuttle, *Buran*, was launched in 1988. This was an unmanned test flight which flew two orbits.

Buran looks like the American shuttles, but is designed to carry up to 10 cosmonauts for a month in space. It is also built to carry larger payloads into orbit.

The Soviet space program includes building another two or three shuttles.

▷ The Soviet shuttle *Buran* about to blast off on Energia, the world's most powerful spacecraft booster.

▽ *Buran*, which means "snowstorm," lands automatically after its first flight.

23

◁ The latest design for the European shuttle *Hermes*.

▽ *Hotol*, a British design for a future spaceplane. This type of craft will take off like an airplane and accelerate to Mach 25 (25 times the speed of sound), the speed needed to reach orbit. One day, spaceplanes may also be used as regular airliners.

Some space shuttles have progressed only to the design stage, while others are no more than ideas. Small shuttles have been planned by ESA and Japan.

ESA plans to launch their shuttle, *Hermes*, in the late 1990s. The Japanese will launch their *Hope* shuttle at about the same time.

Research has begun on the design of spaceplanes, which would take off, as well as land, like an airplane.

Facts

The *Challenger* disaster
Challenger's tenth flight had been scheduled six times, but was delayed due to bad weather and technical problems, before it finally took off on January 28, 1986. Tragically, it lasted only 73 seconds. A defective seal on one of the solid-fuel booster rockets caused an explosion which blew the shuttle apart.

The seven astronauts who died in the disaster were Francis Scobee (commander), Michael Smith (pilot), mission specialists Judith Resnik, Ellison Onizuka and Ronald McNair,

△ *Challenger* on top of the NASA 747 on its way to its first launch. It had made more flights than any other orbiter before it blew up in the 1986 disaster.

Gregory Jarvis (payload specialist) and schoolteacher Christa McAuliffe, the first shuttle passenger in the Teacher in Space program.

Dial-a-Shuttle
A listen-in telephone service is available in the United States that enables callers to hear radio conversations between astronauts and mission control.

Space-to-ground shuttle conversations may also be heard on certain short-wave radio frequencies.

Space camps
Space camps for children have been opened in the United States. They have space-training machines and shuttle simulators. There are three- and five-day programs for 10-14-year-olds.

Longest flight
The longest shuttle flight was made by *Columbia* in 1990. It lasted 10 days, 21 hours and 1 1/2 minutes, a day longer than scheduled because of fog on

the landing site. The number of Earth orbits was 173. Modifications to the shuttle fleet, including extra fuel, oxygen and supplies, will enable shuttles to stay in space for up to 16 days in the 1990s.

Monkey business
Spacelab 3 in the *Challenger* shuttle carried two laboratory monkeys. Their cages were not sufficiently well designed to contain animal feed and droppings, which then floated around the cabin. The crew had to put on surgical masks while vacuuming the air.

△ The flight deck of a NASA space shuttle. The displays and controls are used to pilot the orbiter and to monitor and control its systems. The commander sits on the left, the pilot on the right.

Rocket power
Energia, the rocket that launches Soviet shuttle *Buran* into orbit, is the most powerful in the world. It is capable of lifting 100 tons into space. This is about 10 tons more than the Saturn V rocket, abandoned by NASA in 1973.

Glossary

Airlock
A chamber that astronauts or experiments pass through between the pressurized interior of the shuttle and the outside, which has no pressure.

Commander
The astronaut in overall command of the shuttle. He or she is the chief pilot for all parts of the flight that are not automatically controlled.

Manipulator arm
The maneuverable mechanical arm that can be controlled from inside the shuttle to work in the cargo bay or outside the shuttle. Astronauts also use it when they are outside the shuttle, sometimes as a platform.

Mission specialist
Astronaut trained to operate the shuttle's mission equipment, such as the manipulator arm.

Orbit
The path taken by the shuttle or any other body around a large body such as the Earth.

Orbiter
The shuttle without its external fuel tank and booster rockets.

Payload
A shuttle's cargo, including experiments inside the shuttle or in the cargo bay and anything being placed in orbit.

Payload specialist
Astronaut with responsibility for operating a particular experiment on board the shuttle.

Pilot
The astronaut who sits next to the commander on the flight deck and serves as copilot.

Zero gravity
The condition in space where there is no noticeable pull toward the Earth or any other large body. Everything inside a shuttle in orbit floats freely if not restrained, including the astronauts.

Index

PRINTED IN BELGIUM BY

proost

INTERNATIONAL BOOK PRODUCTION